mommy & me craft

DK

LONDON, NEW YORK, MUNICH,
MELBOURNE, and DELHI

Senior designer Hannah Moore
Editor Jo Casey
US editor Margaret Parrish
Photographer Dave King
Production editor Andy Hilliard
Production controller Ché Creasey
Jacket designer Rosie Levine
Managing editor Penny Smith
Managing art editor Marianne Markham
Creative director Jane Bull
Category publisher Mary Ling

First American Edition, 2013
Published in the United States by
DK Publishing
4th floor, 345 Hudson Street
New York, New York 10014

14 15 16 17 18 10 9 8 7 6 5 4 3 2 1
001-196500-02/14

A catalog record for this book
is available from the Library of Congress.
ISBN: 978-1-4654-1657-5

Printed and bound in China
by Hung Hing

Discover more at
www.dk.com

Contents

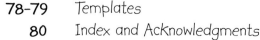

Introduction

In this book you will discover facts about a selection of materials such as yarn and paper. You'll find out where they come from and discover exciting and fun crafts to make with them.

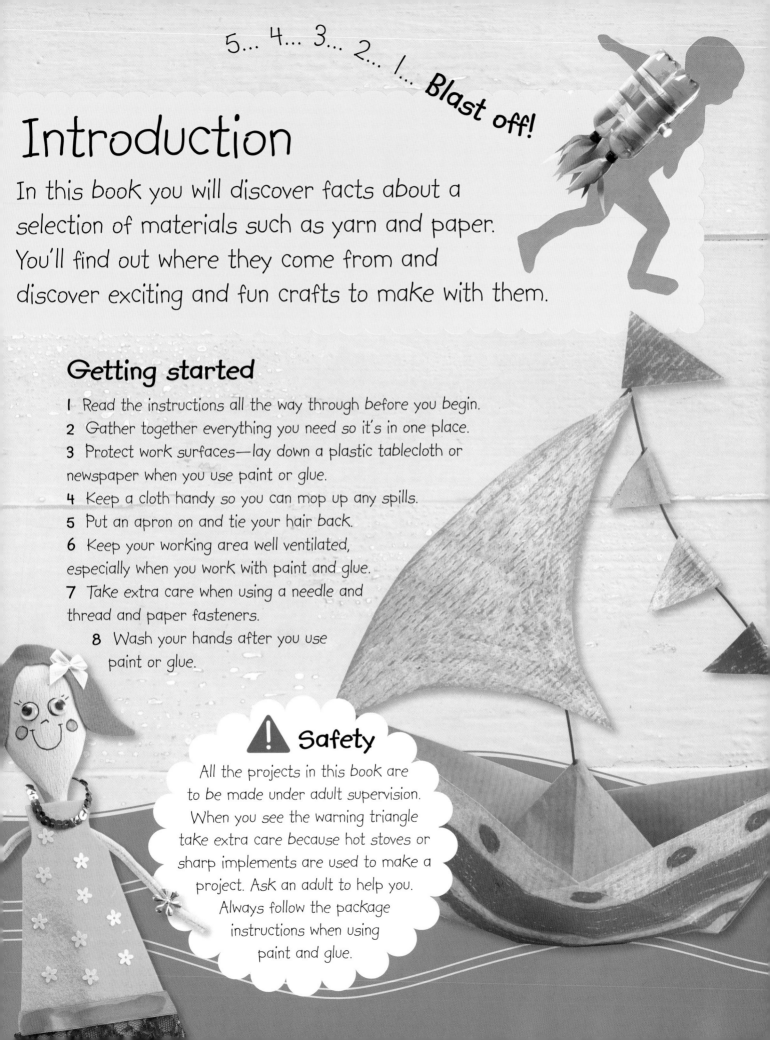

Getting started

1 Read the instructions all the way through before you begin.

2 Gather together everything you need so it's in one place.

3 Protect work surfaces—lay down a plastic tablecloth or newspaper when you use paint or glue.

4 Keep a cloth handy so you can mop up any spills.

5 Put an apron on and tie your hair back.

6 Keep your working area well ventilated, especially when you work with paint and glue.

7 Take extra care when using a needle and thread and paper fasteners.

8 Wash your hands after you use paint or glue.

⚠ Safety

All the projects in this book are to be made under adult supervision. When you see the warning triangle take extra care because hot stoves or sharp implements are used to make a project. Ask an adult to help you. Always follow the package instructions when using paint and glue.

5... 4... 3... 2... 1... Blast off!

Paper is pretty amazing. You can use it to make lots of fun crafts; from beads and boats, to windmills and windsocks!

What is paper?

We use paper to write on, paint on, draw on, and so much more. But have you ever thought about where paper comes from? Paper as we know it doesn't grow on trees, although it is made from trees!

Paper can be **recycled**, which means turning something old into something new.

Recycled paper can be shaped into lots of paper products, such as egg cartons. (Turn to pages 50-51 for a great egg-carton craft!)

Think about how many times you use paper every day. Newspaper, tissue paper, wrapping paper, toilet paper, books, cards, magazines, comic books, money, tracing paper, maps, candy wrappers... paper is everywhere!

How is paper made?

Trees

Trees are cut down and the branches are cut off.

Paper mill

At the paper mill the bark is removed from the logs. The logs are crushed into a mushy pulp and water and chemicals are added.

The water is squeezed from the pulp and then the pulp is rolled flat into paper. The rolls of paper are cut into smaller rolls, ready to be delivered to stores.

Huge rolls of paper

Before the invention of paper, people used stones, animal skins, palm leaves, or fabric to write on.

Paper was invented a long time ago by the ancient Egyptians. They made it from the papyrus plant, which is where paper gets its name.

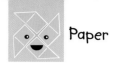
Larry the lion mask

Grab a paper plate, yellow paint, and colored construction paper and make a Larry the lion mask. It's easy to do—just follow the steps and you'll be roaring like a lion in no time!

Ask an adult to help you cut out the templates on page 78.

A female lion is called a lioness. A lioness doesn't have a mane, so don't add raffia ribbon to the edges if you want to make a lioness mask.

If you don't have raffia ribbon, you can use strips of tissue paper instead.

You will need:

tracing paper • pencil • scissors • yellow, beige, brown, and dark brown construction paper • paper plate • yellow acrylic paint • paintbrush • craft glue • raffia ribbon • glue stick • black felt-tip pen • elastic

1 Trace the templates on page 78 onto tracing paper. Cut them out. Place the shapes over construction paper, draw around them, and cut out.

2 Paint the back of the paper plate yellow and let it dry. Cut small triangles three-quarters of the way around the edges of the plate.

3 Position the eyes on the plate and trace around the circles in the middle. Ask an adult to cut out the two circles.

4 Cut strips of raffia ribbon and glue them three-quarters of the way around the edges of the plate. Glue strips of raffia onto the bottom of the plate.

5 To make the nose, fold the widest end under by about ½in (1cm). Fold in half lengthwise and then open it out.

6 Draw dots on the cheeks and glue the ears, eyes, chin, cheeks, and the shortest end of the nose onto the plate.

7 Ask an adult to cut two holes in both sides of the plate. Thread elastic through the holes and tie the ends.

More animal masks

You can make all kinds of animal masks. Would you like to be an exotic bird or a bouncing bunny? Let your imagination run wild!

If you don't have feathers you can use colored tissue paper to make this bright bird mask. Your mask doesn't have to be round—experiment with different shapes.

You can attach your mask to a stick instead of using elastic to tie it around your head.

You need two paper plates, felt, raffia ribbon, white paper, and a pom-pom to make this cute bunny. (Use a ready-made pom-pom or make your own. See pages 26-27 for pom-pom instructions.)

9

Most origami starts with a square piece of paper.

Origami windmill

Wow your friends with this fabulous origami windmill. Pin it to a stick, take it outside, and watch it whirl in the wind.

You will need:

colorful square paper • scissors • stick • thumbtack

Origami is the Japanese art of folding paper to make shapes.

Use candy wrappers to make these cute mini windmills.

1 Fold the square piece of paper in half and unfold.

2 Fold both sides into the middle.

3 Fold the rectangle in half, crease, and unfold. Bring the top and bottom into the middle and fold.

4 Fold the bottom right corner to the top left corner to make a triangle, and unfold. Repeat with the bottom left corner. Unfold the square to make a rectangle.

5 With your forefingers inside the bottom corners, your remaining fingers holding down the middle, and your thumbs underneath, gently pull the corners out to form a boat shape.

6 Press down the middle and crease well.

7 Repeat steps 5-6 for the top corners.

8 Fold the bottom left triangle shape down and then fold the top right corner triangle shape up.

9 Poke your fingers inside all of the four triangles to give them shape.

10 Cut one big circle and one small circle out of paper and place the circles in the middle of the windmill. Ask an adult to pin your windmill to a stick. ⚠

Blow on your windmill and watch it spin!

Fish scale

Fish tail

Fish fin

Fantastic fish windsock

You need to cut out lots of foil and tissue paper scales to make this sparkly fish. Once you have made your fishy friend, take it outside and watch it swim in the breeze!

You will need:

colored foil (cut out 14 semicircles about 3in [7cm] wide) • colored tissue paper (cut out 14 semicircles about 3in [7cm] wide, 8 strips about 20cm [8in] in length, and 4 fin shapes) • scissors • paper towel roll • double-sided tape • glue stick • white paper • black felt-tip pen • stick • string • masking tape

1 Ask an adult to cut a paper towel roll in half. Stick double-sided tape all the way around the inside of one end of the roll.

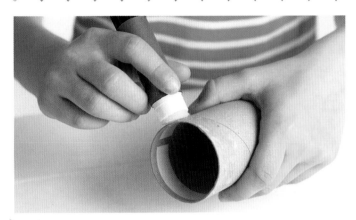

2 Spread glue all around one end of the roll.

3 Glue the tissue paper and foil scales onto the roll, overlapping each scale slightly. Alternate between the tissue paper and the foil scales.

4 Continue spreading glue around the roll and gluing on the scales. Overlap each row slightly until the whole roll is covered.

5 For the fish eyes, draw two small circles onto white paper and cut them out. Draw a black dot in the middle of each circle and glue onto each side of the roll.

6 Stick the fish tails onto the tape inside the tail end of the roll. Then glue two fins onto each side of the roll.

You can also design your own windsock. Take solid-colored paper and use colorful felt-tip pens, pencils, crayons, or paint to make a pattern. Glue the paper onto the roll.

Tie about 2ft (60cm) of string around one end of a stick. Attach both ends of the string inside the top of the roll with masking tape. Take your fish outside and watch it swim!

Only use a little glue or your beads will stick to the knitting needle.

Pretty paper **beads**

Make one-of-a-kind jewelry by rolling triangles of paper into beads. Use a mixture of colors to make pretty necklaces and bracelets. Ready, set... roll!

You can use old catalogs, posters, and wallpaper.

You will need:

magazines, colored paper, or wrapping paper • ruler • pencil • scissors • knitting needle or wooden skewer • glue stick • glitter glue • string • elastic • plastic beads

Coat your finished beads with varnish to make them shiny and strong.

Before you cut out lots of triangles, make one test bead with your chosen paper to see if you like the overall effect.

1 Use a ruler to draw triangles about 1¼in (3cm) wide and 12in (30cm) in length onto paper. Carefully cut out each triangle.

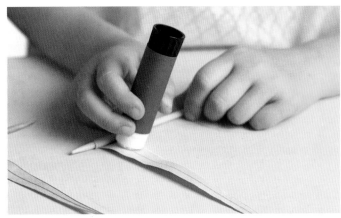

2 Place the needle on the widest end of the triangle and roll the paper around the needle twice. Spread glue along the rest of the triangle.

3 Continue rolling the needle to the end of the triangle, pressing down firmly as you roll.

4 Slide the bead off the needle and let it dry. Before beginning your next bead wipe the needle (and your hands!) clean of glue.

5 Once your beads are dry, squirt a dollop of glitter glue onto scrap paper. Roll each bead in it to create a fabulous sparkly effect.

6 Once you start making paper beads it will be hard to stop! Make lots and then turn the page to find out how to make a fantastic bracelet.

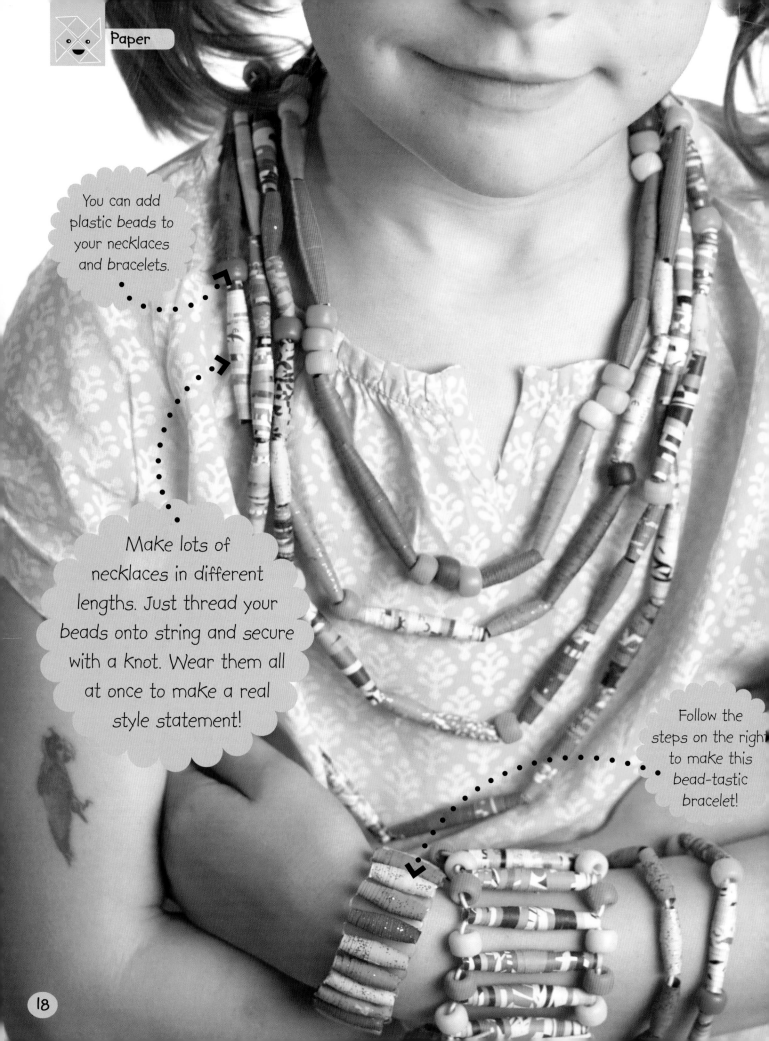

You can add plastic beads to your necklaces and bracelets.

Make lots of necklaces in different lengths. Just thread your beads onto string and secure with a knot. Wear them all at once to make a real style statement!

Follow the steps on the right to make this bead-tastic bracelet!

Bead-tastic bracelet

1 Fold a length of elastic in half and check that it will fit around your wrist. Thread one end through one side of a bead and thread the other end through the opposite side of the bead.

2 Pull both ends of elastic until the bead reaches the end of the loop.

3 Continue adding beads onto the elastic in this way. Stop when you are near the end of the elastic.

4 To finish, thread one end of elastic through the first bead you started with. Thread the other end of elastic through the opposite side of the same bead. Tie the ends in a double knot.

Homemade paste

If you don't have wallpaper paste you can make your own. Ask an adult to follow the steps below. You will need 1 cup of all-purpose flour and 3 cups of water.

1 Put 1 cup of water and 1 cup of flour into a saucepan and stir until the mixture is smooth.

2 Add the rest of the water and bring to a boil, stirring all the time.

3 Pour the mixture into a bowl and let it cool.

Ollie the octopus

Use old newspapers to make new things, like Ollie the paper-mache octopus. Octopuses usually live in the ocean, but Ollie would be more than happy to live in your bedroom!

You will need:

scissors • newspapers • red tissue paper • inflated balloon • masking tape • jar • petroleum jelly • paintbrush • homemade paste or wallpaper paste • garden wire • white paper • black felt-tip pen • craft glue • blue tissue paper (cut out about 60 small circles)

Get ready! Cut out lots of newspaper squares and strips and red tissue-paper squares.

1 Tape the *balloon* on top of the jar and rub petroleum jelly all over it. Use the brush to paste on the newspaper squares. Continue pasting them on until you have about four layers.

2 Put the *balloon* aside to dry. Ask an adult to cut 8 pieces of garden wire about 10in (25cm) long and shape them into tentacles. Use masking tape to hold the tentacle shapes in place.

3 Attach the tentacles to the *balloon* with masking tape. Brush the newspaper strips with paste. Wrap them around each tentacle until they are all covered.

4 Next, paste the tissue paper squares all over the *balloon* and tentacles until they are completely covered.

Glue the eyes onto Ollie.

5 For the eyes, cut two oval shapes about 4in (10cm) long and 3in (7cm) wide from white paper. Color in black pupils.

6 Glue the tissue paper circles all over the balloon and tentacles. Set aside to dry.

7 You're almost finished! Turn the *balloon* upside down, snip the Knot, and remove the balloon.

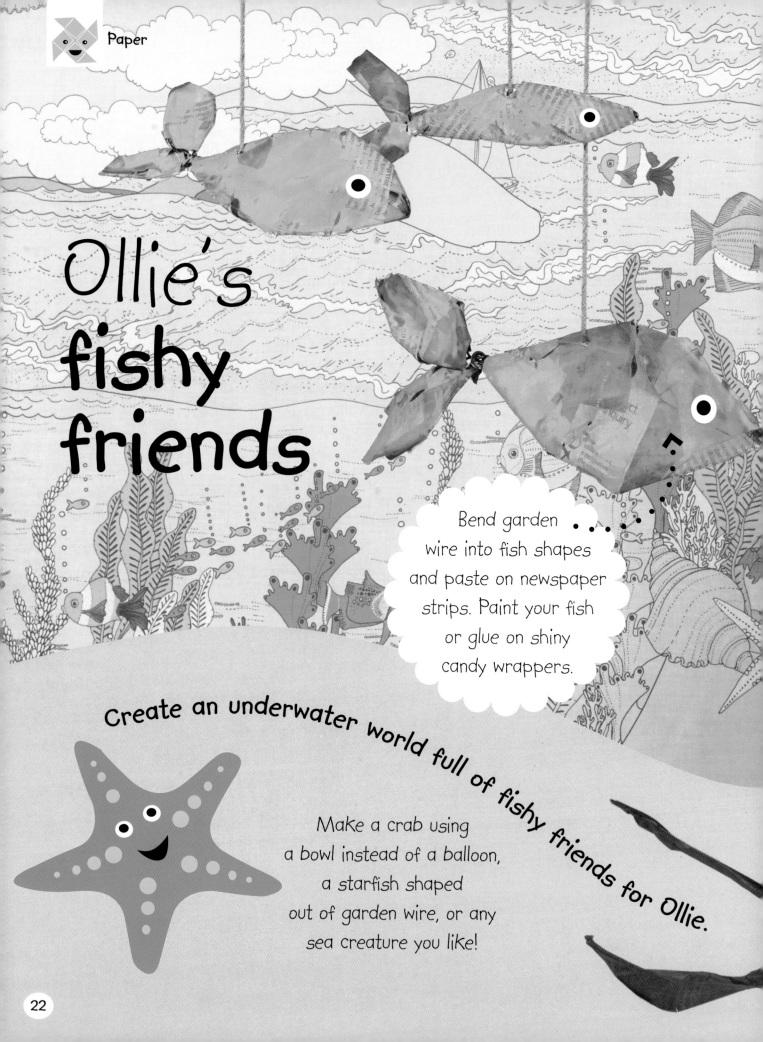

Ollie's fishy friends

Bend garden wire into fish shapes and paste on newspaper strips. Paint your fish or glue on shiny candy wrappers.

Create an underwater world full of fishy friends for Ollie.

Make a crab using a bowl instead of a balloon, a starfish shaped out of garden wire, or any sea creature you like!

Ask an adult to make a hole through the top of Ollie. Thread yarn through the hole at the bottom and out of the hole at the top and hang Ollie from a shelf.

Magazines, comic books, candy wrappers, junk mail, and envelopes can all be used to make a paper mache project!

Female sheep are called ewe and males are called rams. Baby sheep are lambs.

What is yarn?

Yarn is often made of wool, which comes from sheep and has been used for thousands of years to make clothes that keep us warm and dry. Wool is very smart stuff—water runs off it and it's difficult to set on fire, making it a useful material in firefighters' clothes.

Up to eight wool sweaters can be made from one fleece (a sheep's coat).

You won't find a sheep with a bright pink fleece! Wool absorbs dye easily and can be dyed into beautiful colors.

Wool is good for the planet because it is biodegradable. This means that it can be broken down easily without harming the environment.

A good shearer takes less than **five** minutes to shear a sheep.

Every spring, sheep get a dramatic haircut and their fleeces are shorn. The fleece is removed in one single piece by a shearer. The shearer must hold a sheep in place and not cut its skin.

The wool is washed to remove any stains and then it goes through a carding machine, which combs the wool to remove all the dirt.

Raw wool is soft and fluffy!

Most wool is spun on big machines, but some people still spin wool by hand, using a spinning wheel.

A modern factory spinning machine pulls and twists the wool tightly into long strands, called yarn. Then it's ready for knitting!

Wool yarn can be the natural color of the sheep it came from or it can be dyed to any color.

Fluffy pom-poms

Make these cute balls of fluff by using scraps of yarn that are too short for knitting. Making pom-poms is so fun that chances are once you make one you simply won't be able to stop!

Get ready! Cut two matching disks of cardboard with holes in the middle. Then cut slits like these through the edges.

You will need:

cardboard • pencil • scissors • yarn • fabric glue • mini pom-poms • googly eyes

The size of your disks determines the size of your pom-pom. About 4in (10cm) wide is a good size.

1 Put one cardboard disk on top of the other and tie the end of the yarn around both.

2 Wind the yarn around and around the disks, through the middle and over the top. The more yarn you use, the fatter your pom-pom will be.

3 Slip the scissors between the disks and carefully snip the yarn all the way around, holding the disks firmly.

4 Wrap a piece of yarn between the disks. Pull the yarn tight and tie in a knot to hold the yarn in place.

5 Gently pull the disks off the pom-pom. Trim the ends of the long piece of yarn.

6 Fluff up your pom-pom and snip all around it to neaten it up. Glue the mini pom-poms and googly eyes in place to finish your pom-pom.

Pom-pom creatures

You can craft your pom-poms into all kinds of weird and wonderful creatures. Just gather together felt, googly eyes, and cardboard and start creating!

Squeak, squeak! Braid strands of yarn to make a tail for this sweet pom-pom mouse.

Glue a small pom-pom onto a bigger pom-pom using fabric glue to make this cute bunny.

If you don't have felt use colored construction paper instead. Cut out the shapes and glue them on with craft glue.

Use colorful feathers to make this adorable pom-pom bird.

Create a monster pom-pom using a pipe cleaner for antennae and felt for feet.

Paper plate **weaving**

With just a paper plate and scraps of colorful yarn you can make a wonderful weave. Turn your finished weave into a bright coaster or a pretty wall hanging, or put it in a picture frame to display it.

If you don't have an embroidery needle you can use a large paper clip instead.

You will need:
paper plate
• pencil • ruler
• scissors • skewer
• embroidery needle
• yarn

String, plastic bags, and old T-shirts cut into strips also make great weaving materials!

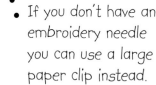

When you have finished weaving, cut each strand and tie it in a knot.

A paper plate in any size will do.

You can also weave with a plastic drink stirrer.

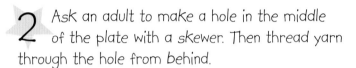

1 Using a ruler, divide the plate into 16 equal segments. Carefully cut out 16 triangle shapes all around the edge of the plate.

2 Ask an adult to make a hole in the middle of the plate with a skewer. Then thread yarn through the hole from behind.

3 Hook the yarn over a segment and back under through the hole. Repeat this on all the segments and then tie a knot at the back.

4 Cut a short length of yarn and tie two of the strands together to make 15 segments. Now you're ready to weave!

5 Thread a needle with yarn and thread the yarn through the hole from behind. Place the needle under a strand, then over the next strand. Continue to thread over and under, all around the plate.

6 To change yarn color, tie the end of the new piece of yarn onto the end of the last piece of yarn you used. Tuck the strands under the weave. When you've covered the plate, tie the end of the yarn to a strand and tuck it under your weave.

Scale it up!

Take weaving to another level by working with a hula hoop. Chunky yarn works best for a massive weave— double up each piece of yarn to make it even chunkier and then start weaving!

over

under

over

under

over

Your finished hula hoop weave can be used as a comfy rug or you can make two and stitch them together to make a pillow cover—it will brighten up any room!

How to hula hoop weave

1 Begin by looping eight pieces of evenly spaced yarn around the hula hoop. Tie each piece of yarn in a knot.

2 Use tape to secure each loop to the hoop.

3 Tie one loop together with a piece of yarn to create 15 loops, as you did with your paper plate.

4 Thread a large paper clip with yarn and begin threading the yarn under and over each loop.

5 When you are finished weaving, cut each loop and tie it in a knot.

The stitching is done on these pegs.

Any colorful yarn will do, but try to use up leftover yarn—it's perfect for making long, striped cords.

Knitting doll

This clever doll is very good at knitting. With your help, she produces pretty cords that can be made into beautiful items for you and your friends.

Use a knitting pin to lift the yarn over the pegs.

As if by magic, gorgeous knitted cord comes out of the bottom of the d

You will need:

colorful yarn • knitting doll • knitting pin • scissors

⭐1 Thread the yarn down through the center of the doll, leaving about 4in (10cm) of yarn out of the bottom. Wrap the yarn around the first peg.

⭐2 Next, wrap the yarn around the second, third, and fourth pegs.

⭐3 Lay the yarn across the outside of the first peg.

⭐4 Now you're ready to knit! Use the knitting pin to pull out the bottom loop from the first peg.

⭐5 Lift the loop over the peg and the stitch is complete. Continue to lay the yarn across the outside of each peg and lift each stitch over it.

⭐6 Pull on the yarn at the end as you complete each stitch. Slowly, the knitted cord will appear out of the bottom of the doll.

Casting off

⭐1 Lift the last stitch you made onto the peg next to it, pull out the bottom loop, and lift the loop over the peg.

⭐2 Repeat step one until just one loop remains.

⭐3 Lift up the loop with your pin and enlarge it with the pin.

⭐4 To finish, cut the thread, pass it through the loop, and pull it tight. Tie a knot to secure it.

Cute creations

You won't get bored making cute creations with your knitted cord. Purses, petals, or pen jars—you can make plenty of things!

Coil flower

1 Roll about 4½in (11cm) of cord into a coil. Use pins to secure the coil shape and then stitch it together at the back. Remove the pins after stitching.

2 For the petals, knit about 22in (55cm) of cord. Pin each petal shape to the coil and then stitch in place at the back. Remove the pins after stitching.

You can sew a brooch pin to the back of your flowers and pin them to a hat or a jacket.

Pen pot

Use up scraps of yarn to knit long, colorful cord. Ask an adult to glue the cord around a glass jar. You can use your jazzed-up jar to hold your paintbrushes and pencils.

Button flower

1 You will need to knit about 16in (40cm) of cord to make these button flowers. Fold the cord into a flower shape, using pins to hold the shape in place.

2 Stitch the petal shapes together at the back. Remove the pins after stitching.

3 Sew a bright button in the middle of your flower.

This little purse is a project to do over time because you will need to knit lots and lots of cord to make it. You will be so pleased with the result that all of your work will have been worth it!

Sew on a button and a fastening loop to keep your things safe.

Pretty purse

1 Knit two pieces of cord just over 5ft (160cm) long. Roll one cord into a coil and use pins to hold the shape in place.

2 Sew the coil together at the back. This will be on the inside of the purse. Remove the pins after sewing. Repeat with the other cord.

3 Place one unstitched side of a coil on top of the unstitched side of the other coil. Sew the two together around the edges, leaving the top unstitched. Turn the purse inside out so all the stitching is on the inside.

4 Knit another piece of cord for the strap. It can be as long or as short as you like. Place both ends of the cord inside the top of the bag and sew in place.

What is paint?

Imagine a world without paint—it would be a very dull place! People have been using paint to color everything from caves, pictures, and buildings for thousands of years.

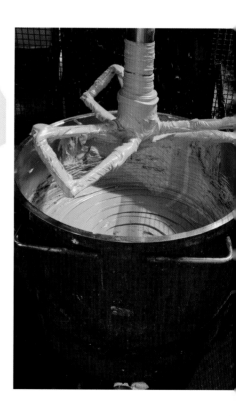

How is paint made?

The two main ingredients in paint are "pigment," which gives paint its color, and "binder," which gives paint its texture. Pigment and binder are mixed together and then poured into a milling machine, which spreads the pigments evenly.

Pigments are crushed into a fine powder.

Start with some beautiful **pigments**... mix each pigment with **binder**

Red ocher is a natural pigment found in the soil. Cavemen mixed it with dirt, saliva, or animal fat to create paint.

Cave paintings The first paintings were created on cave walls. Paintbrushes didn't exist, so fingertips, moss, twigs, feathers, and hollow bones were used.

If you run out of your favorite paint, don't despair! Did you know that if you mix two primary colors (red, yellow, or blue) together they make a completely different color?

 purple

+ = orange

+ = green

... put the paint mixture into a **tube**... and then have **fun!**

Sticker
T-shirt

Masking
tape
T-shirt

Design a T-shirt

Take a solid-colored T-shirt and transform it into
a true original. All you need is tape, stickers,
paint, and a bit of imagination!

Use stickers that have
interesting shapes,
like these stars.

You will need:

solid-colored T-shirt • maskir
tape • scissors • fabric pair
• sponges • stickers • iron

Use a solid-colo
T-shirt in any co

Cut sponges into cubes
squirt paint into a foil
tray, and start dabbing

Masking tape T-shirt

1 Lay the T-shirt flat and stick strips of masking tape onto the T-shirt in any design you like.

2 Using a sponge, dab fabric paint on and around the pieces of masking tape.

3 Let the paint dry and then carefully peel off the pieces of masking tape.

4 Turn the T-shirt inside out and ask an adult to iron over the design to fix it in place.

Sticker T-shirt

1 Apply the stickers to the T-shirt in any way you like.

2 Dab fabric paint on and around the stickers with a sponge and let dry.

3 Peel off the stickers. Turn the T-shirt inside out and ask an adult to iron over the design.

41

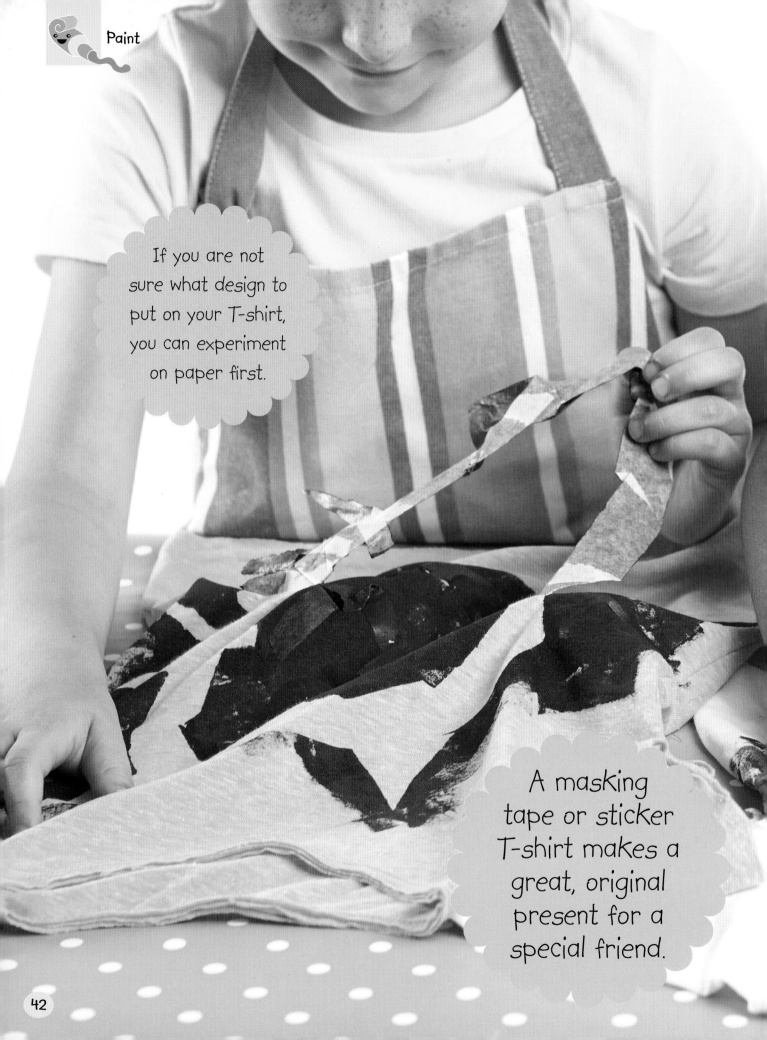

If you are not sure what design to put on your T-shirt, you can experiment on paper first.

A masking tape or sticker T-shirt makes a great, original present for a special friend.

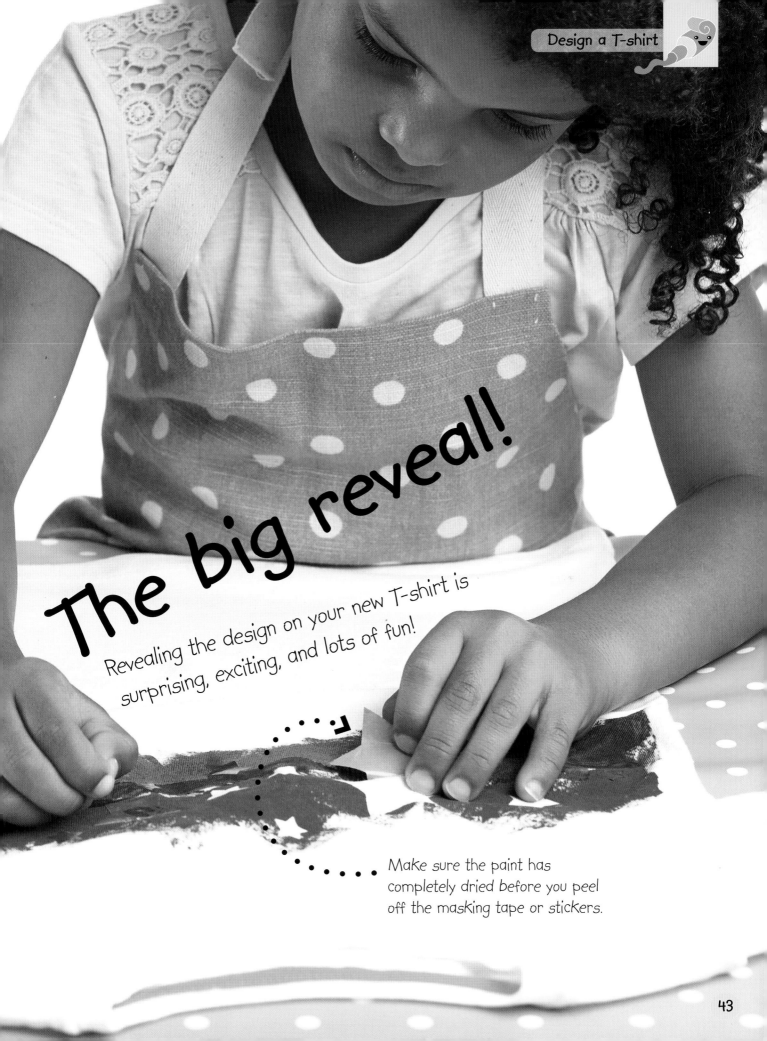

The big reveal!

Revealing the design on your new T-shirt is surprising, exciting, and lots of fun!

Make sure the paint has completely dried before you peel off the masking tape or stickers.

43

If you don't live near a beach, you can buy stones in most craft stores.

Painted stones

Transform stones into fabulous works of art! You can turn them into bugs or butterflies or cover them in patterns. Display them on your desk, shelves, or use them as paperweights.

Use fine felt-tip pens or paintbrushes to add details to your stones.

You will need:

clean, dry stones • acrylic paints • paintbrushes • clear varnish or craft glue • felt-tip pens

Choose colorful acrylic paints, then start painting

1 You can paint any design you like, but for a lovely ladybug follow these steps. Paint the stone all over with a *base* color. Your design will really stand out on white paint.

2 Once the *base paint* is dry, paint three-quarters of the stone red and let it dry.

3 Paint the remainder of the stone black and add a black line down the middle. Don't forget to give your ladybug black spots, two white eyes with *black* dots in the middle, and a red smile!

4 When the paint is completely dry, cover it with varnish to make it nice and shiny. If you don't have varnish you can mix craft glue with a little water instead.

Polystyrene prints

Pizza packaging is a good base for your prints.

Pretty prints, cute prints, crazy prints, funny prints—whatever mood you're in, you can create an amazing polystyrene print to match it!

A pussy cat print is a purr-fect present to give to someone special!

1 Draw a picture on a piece of paper with a felt-tip pen—simple designs work best. Lay the paper over the polystyrene and trace over the drawing with a *ballpoint* pen, pressing down hard.

2 Check that the pen indentation is fairly deep on the polystyrene. If it isn't, draw over the picture again.

4 With a roller, spread paint evenly all over your picture. Don't put too much paint on or you will end up with a *big goop* of paint!

5 Place colored paper over the polystyrene and firmly press down on it with your hands

You can print portraits of your family and friends!

Use a ballpoint pen to add texture to the polystyrene. This will make your finished print more interesting!

Carefully peel the paper off to reveal your fabulous print!

You will need:

white paper • felt-tip pen • polystyrene packaging • ballpoint pen • acrylic paint • roller • colored paper

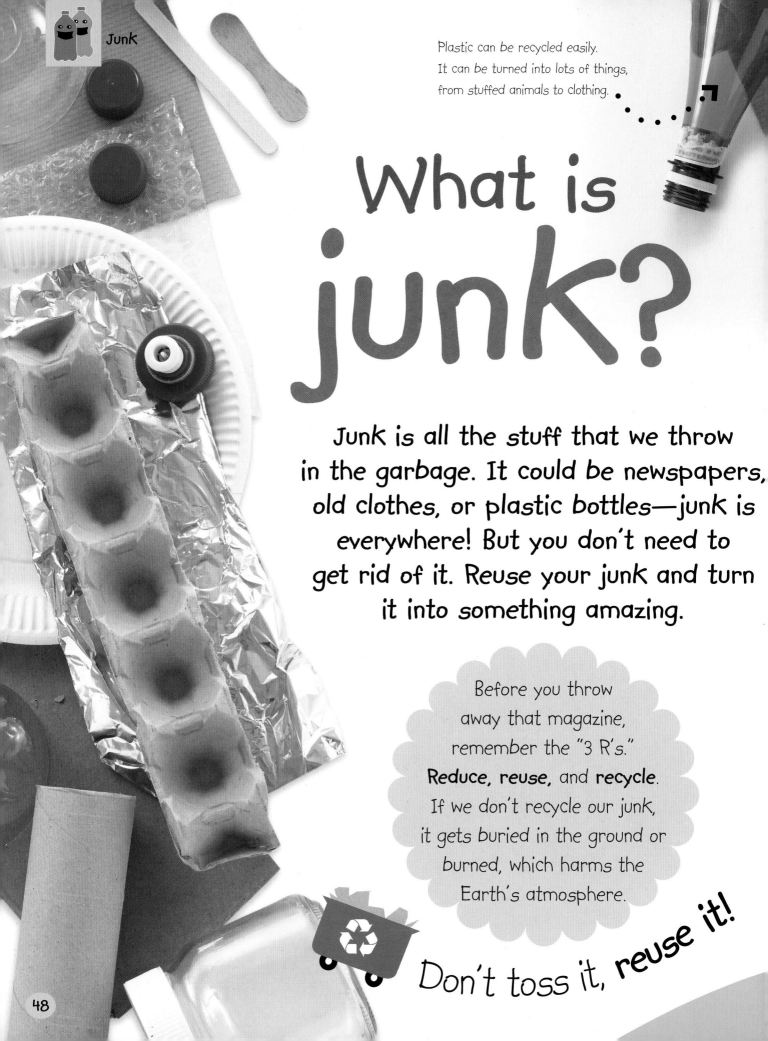

Plastic can be recycled easily. It can be turned into lots of things, from stuffed animals to clothing.

What is junk?

Junk is all the stuff that we throw in the garbage. It could be newspapers, old clothes, or plastic bottles—junk is everywhere! But you don't need to get rid of it. Reuse your junk and turn it into something amazing.

Before you throw away that magazine, remember the "3 R's." **Reduce, reuse,** and **recycle.** If we don't recycle our junk, it gets buried in the ground or burned, which harms the Earth's atmosphere.

Don't toss it, reuse it!

What junk can we reuse?

Fabric is fabulous. Some fabrics, such as wool, come from animals. Other fabrics, such as Lycra, are made in a laboratory. Don't throw out that old T-shirt— transform it!

Fabric

Plastic is fantastic. Plastic is made with a substance called cellulose, which comes from the wood pulp of trees. It can take hundreds of years for plastic to disappear from the Earth—so reuse it!

Plastic

Glass

Paper

Metal

Glass is great. But the fact that it takes over one million years to break down isn't. Turn to page 60 to discover how you can reuse glass.

Turn to page 60 to discover how you can reuse glass.

Paper is perfect for crafting! When we reuse old paper, fewer tress have to be cut down to make new paper.

Metal is marvelous. Metal comes from rocks, which are broken up and heated, releasing the metal. Reusing metal is good for the environment.

Reusing your junk will help **save the planet!**

Sammy the snake

This is Sammy the snake, and he is made from egg cartons. Egg cartons can be used to create all kinds of egg-cellent creatures. It's time to get cracking with this craft!

You will need:

cardboard egg cartons • scissors • green and yellow poster paint • paintbrush • skewer • embroidery needle • string • beads • red felt • craft glue • googly eyes • two sticks

⚠

1 Ask an adult to help you cut the lids off the egg cartons and cut off each segment. You will need about 26 segments to make Sammy.

4 Thread string through one segment and tie knot at the end of the string. Next, thread bead onto the string, followed by another segment Repeat with the rest of the segments.

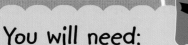

You will need about 20in (50cm) of string to make Sammy.

Hold the two sticks in your hands

Paint 16 segments with the green poster paint and 10 segments with the yellow poster paint. t aside to dry.

3 Ask an adult to make a hole through the middle of each segment with a skewer. Always point the skewer away from your body.

Leave about 1½in (3cm) of string at the end and tie a knot. Next, give Sammy features! t a tongue shape out of red felt and glue it onto e string. Add two googly eyes.

6 Tie two pieces of string around the top and bottom half of the snake and attach each piece of string to a stick.

e Sammy dance!

You can use cardboard, pom-poms, and garden wire to make more cute egg-carton critters.

Spoon dolly

Wooden spoons aren't just for stirring—
they can also become spectacular spoon dollies!
Gather scraps of felt, fabric, trimmings,
and sparkly sequins to decorate your dolls.

You can craft a spoon
of someone you know,
or even one of yourself!

You will need:

tracing paper • pencil
• scissors • felt • pins
• ribbon • lace • craft glue
• sequins • wooden spoon
• tape • pipe cleaner
• black felt-tip pen
• googly eyes

Any scraps of colorful
felt will work.

1 Trace the felt shapes (see page 79) onto paper and cut out the shapes. Pin the paper shapes to the felt and cut around them.

2 Cut a piece of ribbon and lace about 5in (12cm) long and glue onto the bottom of the dress. Squirt dabs of glue onto the dress and glue on sequins.

3 Spread glue onto the spoon and glue the felt hair and the front of the dress to the spoon.

4 For the arms, cut a length of pipe cleaner about 8in (20cm) long and tape onto the back of the spoon. Attach the back of the dress with glue.

5 Next, give your spoon a face! Use glue to affix googly eyes, then draw a nose, mouth, and rosy cheeks.

6 Glue sparkly accessories onto the pipe cleaner arm and around the neck. Hook the felt handbag onto the pipe-cleaner arm.

Don't throw takeout spoons away—just wash them and then transform them!

Use scraps of yarn as hair for your spoon dollies.

Cut out felt to make cute outfits.

A baking case folded in half makes a pretty skirt.

Glue buttons onto a doily to fashion a dainty dress.

Super-duper spoon show!

It's showtime! Take a look at these spoons for inspiration and make a whole cast of colorful spoons. Then put on a spectacular spoon show to entertain your family and friends.

Use frilly trimmings to make a fancy dress and feathers for a fabulous hat!

This cool popsicle-stick dude is wearing a candy-wrapper hat.

Make a stage to display your spoons. Wrap boxes with colorful paper and ask an adult to cut slits in the top.

Origami **boat**

These beautiful boats can be made from all types of paper: from magazines and maps, to candy wrappers and wallpaper. Make lots of boats and then turn the page to discover what you can do with them all!

You will need:
letter-sized colored or patterned paper

All aboard this beautiful boat craft!

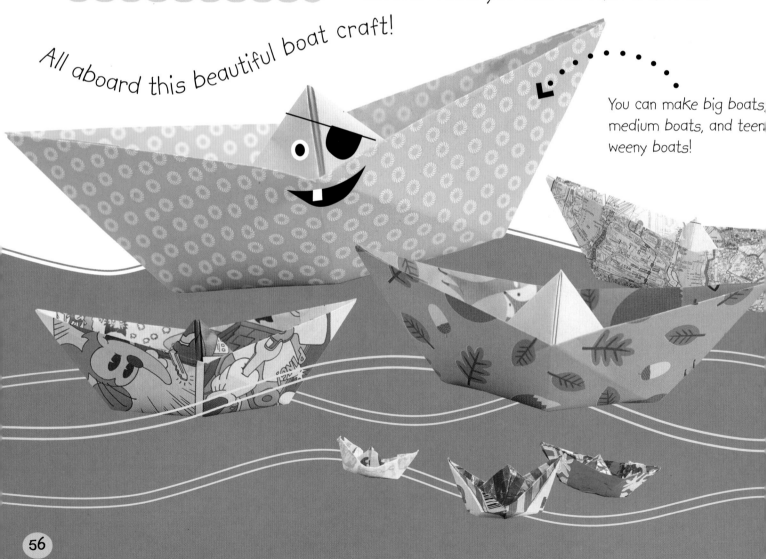

You can make big boats, medium boats, and teeny weeny boats!

1 Start with letter-sized paper, patterned- or colored-side up. Fold in half.

2 Fold in half again, make a crease, and then unfold.

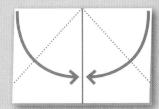

3 Fold both corners in to the center to make a triangle shape.

4 Fold the flap up.

5 Fold both corners behind the triangle and then turn it over.

6 Fold the flap up.

7 Poke your fingers inside to open the triangle out and then flatten down the right side to make a diamond shape.

8 Fold the bottom point of the diamond up to the top point. Turn it over and repeat so that you have a triangle shape.

9 Poke your fingers inside to open the triangle out and then flatten down the right side to make a diamond shape.

10 Take the upper corners of the diamond and pull them out (see the images on the right) to reveal your beautiful boat!

1 Give your origami boats more of a shape by creasing the corners and poking the underneath with your fingers so that they can stand upright.

2 Thread about 3ft (90cm) of yarn through the middle of the boat and tie a knot near the end to secure it.

3 Tie another knot halfway up the yarn and then thread another boat. Repeat steps 1-3 with 3 pieces of yarn, threading 2 boats on each piece of yarn.

4 Make a cross shape with two sticks and wrap about 7ft (240cm) of yarn around the middle to secure them together.

5 Next, wrap each piece of yarn with the boats attached around the edges of each stick and secure with a knot.

6 To make sails, cut diamond shapes from colored paper and fold in half. Use glue to stick the sails to the yarn.

Wrap yarn around the middle of the sticks and hang your mobile from a shelf.

Boat mobile

This colorful boat mobile is the perfect way to show off your boats in all their glory!

You will need:

8 origami boats • embroidery needle • yarn • scissors • 2 sturdy sticks • colored paper • glue stick

You can also design your own boat. Use plain brown paper, garden wire, and chalk.

Snow globe

Raid your toy box for a plastic toy that will fit comfortably inside a glass jar and make a snow globe. A snow globe is the perfect way to display a favorite toy treasure.

Adding a teaspoon of glycerine to the water will thicken it, creating a snowfall effect with the glitter.

⚠️ 1 Ask an adult to glue a stone onto the inside the lid to give your toy height. Glue your toy onto the stone. If you don't want to use a stone, glue the toy directly onto the lid. Set aside to dry

⚠️ 4 To make sure water doesn't leak out, ask an adult to spread strong glue onto the inner rim of the jar lid and screw it on tightly.

Use felt that goes well with your plastic toy. This dino is surrounded by green felt that looks like grass.

You can use a photo

⚠️ 2 Cut a piece of posterboard to the length of your jar and decorate in any way you like. Cover both sides of the posterboard with tape. Use your fingers to remove air bubbles on the tape so water doesn't seep through.

3 Place the posterboard inside the jar and pour in water, almost to the top. Add a teaspoon of glycerine and a teaspoon of glitter.

⚠️ 5 Cut a piece of felt to wrap around your jar. Cut curves on the top edge of the felt and glue on sequins to decorate. Glue the felt onto the jar and let dry.

6 Shake your jar and watch the glittery magic within!

You will need:

stone • glass jar with lid • strong glue
• plastic toy • scissors • posterboard • tape
• water • glycerine • glitter • felt • sequins

...meone special as a background for your snow globe.

61

5... 4... 3... 2... 1... Blast off!

Jet pack

Do you want to blast off into space? Then you need this jet pack! Rinse out two plastic bottles, follow the steps, and get ready for a space adventure.

You will need:

red, yellow, and orange tissue paper • scissors • 2 plastic bottles • duct tape • cardboard • embroidery needle • elastic • black, yellow, and red electrical tape • 2 bottle tops • gray electrical tape • craft glue

You can add more controls to your jet pack with bottle tops and pieces of silver tin foil.

Get ready! Cut out 18 flame shapes, about 7in (18cm) long, from the red, yellow, and orange tissue paper.

Cut a piece of cardboard about 6½in (16cm) wide and 10in (25cm) in length.

1 Wrap 2 strips of duct tape around each bottle. Line up the bottles so that the strips are side-by-side. Wrap 2 strips of duct tape around both bottles to bind them together.

2 Cover the cardboard base with strips of duct tape. Ask an adult to make holes in each corner and thread elastic through the holes to make arm loops. Secure the end with a knot.

3 Lay a strip of duct tape about 14in (35cm) long near the bottom of the base, sticky side up. Stick it down with 2 strips of duct tape.

4 Place the bottles onto the base and stick both sides of the long strip of duct tape to the side of each bottle.

5 Lay out 9 flames and place a strip of electrical tape along the top of the flames. Wrap the tape with the flames attached around the bottle top. Repeat with the remaining flames and the other bottle top.

6 Wrap yellow and red electrical tape around the middle of the 2 strips of duct tape. Then tape 2 bottle tops together with gray electrical tape and glue onto the side of the bottle.

Alien junkship

Is it a bird? Is it a plane? No, it's the amazing alien junkship! Your awesome felt aliens need to travel in an equally awesome spaceship. The best thing about this ship is that it's made from junk!

See pages 70-71 to find out how to make these friendly aliens.

You will need:

strips of tin foil • scissors • plastic bottle • paper bowl • pencil • glue stick • tape • adhesive putty • two felt-tip pen lids • clear dome-shaped cup lid • electrical tape • strong glue • bottle tops

Glue a glue top onto the inside of bottle top to make a cool control for your junkship!

You can also use a clear plastic pot if you don't have a dome-shaped cup lid

Get ready! Cut lots of strips of tin foil to cover the edges of a paper bowl.

1 Ask an adult to cut off the bottom of a plastic bottle. Place it inside the paper bowl and draw a circle around it.

2 Ask an adult to cut out the circle. Spread the glue stick onto the strips of tin foil and glue them all around the side of the bowl.

3 Attach the bottom of the bottle to the inside of the bowl with strips of tape. Turn the bowl over.

4 Put adhesive putty inside the bottle end and stick two felt-tip pen lids on it. Now your felt aliens have seats where they can perch!

5 Attach the cup lid to the bowl with a strip of electrical tape on the inside and on the outside of the lid.

6 Use the strong glue to glue four bottle tops around the sides of the bowl.

7 Finally, place two of your felt alien pals onto the pen lids inside the junkship.

Alien invasion

You can make alien junkships for all of your felt aliens using paper bowls. Paint the bowls different colors and decorate them with construction paper.

Beam us up, Stux!

Room for a little one?

Make lots of junkships and create your own alien invasion!

And me!

Felt is used to make bags, hats, and slippers because it's **strong and lig**

What is felt?

Felt is made from wool, but it isn't spun or woven like yarn or fabric. It's squashed! Felt is a perfect material for crafts because it is easy to sew and cut, and it doesn't unravel.

Turn to pages 70-71 to find out how to make an awesome felt alien!

Felt is a very old material.
For thousands of years it has been used to make a variety of things—from carpets and clothes, to shoes and saddles.

Raw wool

Heat and moisture

Rollers squash the wool

Clean wool

The wool moves along the conveyor belt.

Felt ...

How is felt made? Raw wool is cleaned and then it goes through a machine, where heat and moisture are applied. Rollers squash the material flat, pressing the fibers together, producing felt.

Working with felt used to be a risky business! Hats made with felt were treated with a substance called mercury. Mercury could poison the hatmaker and cause uncontrollable shaking and loss of memory...

... and that's where the saying **"mad as a hatter"** is thought to have originated!

Felt is traditionally used to make yurts, a type of tent, because it is water-resistant, strong, and retains heat.

Awesome aliens

The felt aliens have landed on Earth! But don't worry, these friendly Martians come in peace. Use up scraps of felt to make them and then pop them on top of your pencils.

You don't have to use these exact colors of felt.

You will need:

tracing paper • pencil • scissors • colored felt • pins • embroidery thread • needle

Make Zork's alien bud

Zork

Get ready! Use this template to trace Zork's felt shapes individually onto paper and cut them out.

body x 2

Actual size template

70

1 Pin the paper shapes onto felt and carefully cut around them.

2 Position the *black circle* onto the white circle, and secure it to the pink body with about five stitches.

3 Sew on the tooth using two rows of *backstitch* (*see page 80*). Next, sew on the blue strip using cross-stitch (*see page 80*).

4 Start sewing around the side of the body using running stitch (*see page 80*). Place the arms and the ears in between the pink body pieces. Sew them in as you go along.

5 Leave the bottom of Zork open so that you can put him on top of your pencil.

...y are out of this world!.

Morg

Gorky

Once you've made Zork, you can create your own aliens. Use Zork's buddies as inspiration or make your aliens as weird and wacky as you like!

Stux

Flim

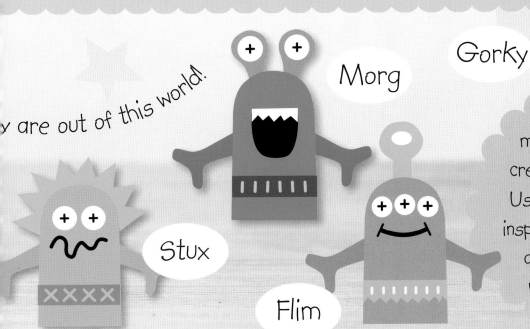

Gold medal

Make this marvelous felt medal and then give it to someone special who is your "Number One." Or, if you've been on your best behavior, you can wear it with pride yourself!

Use a piece of ribbon that fits comfortably around your neck.

Who will be awarded your gold medal?

1 Pin one circle to orange felt, one to white felt, and one to yellow felt. Pin the smaller circle to orange felt. Carefully cut around each circle.

4 Use blanket stitch (see page 80) to attach the yellow circle to the white and orange circles.

You will need:

tracing paper • pencil
• compass • scissors
• felt • pins • embroidery
needle • embroidery
thread • ribbon

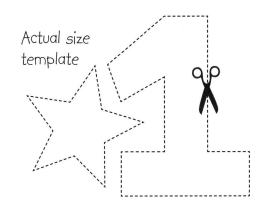

Actual size
template

Get ready! Trace these templates onto paper. Use a compass to draw 3 circles 4in (10cm) in width and a smaller circle 3in (8cm) in width onto paper. Pin each shape to felt and cut around it.

2 Use running stitch (see page 80) to sew the white number one and the white star to the orange circle.

3 Use running stitch to sew the orange circle to the yellow circle.

5 Cut a piece of ribbon that is long enough to go around your neck and fold it in half. Use running stitch to sew the ribbon to the back of the medal.

Once you've made the gold medal, make this rosette or design a badge of your own. Sew a pin back onto the back and wear it on your shirt.

73

Chirp, chirp!

Bean bag bird

You can also use feathers to decorate your bean bags.

This bean bag bird is bags of fun to make and play with. You will need to use basic sewing skills to put it together. Then you can play catch with it, juggle it, display it, or cuddle it!

Make lots of birds in different colors and play the bean bag game on the next page.

You can glue the fabric and felt pieces to the bean bag if you don't want to use running stitch.

Get ready! For the felt rectangle body, cut a piece of felt about 8in (20cm) in width and 16in (40cm) in length.

You will need:
tracing paper • scissors • pins • colored felt • scrap of fabric • needle • embroidery thread • rice • button

1 Trace the felt and fabric shapes (see page 79) onto paper and cut them out. Pin the paper shapes to the felt and fabric and cut around them.

2 Fold the felt rectangle in half. Sew along one short side and the long side using blanket stitch (see page 80).

3 Carefully pour the rice into the opening, about two-thirds of the way to the top.

4 Pinch the sides of the opening together to make a triangle shape. Sew along the opening using blanket stitch.

5 Use running stitch to sew the felt heart crest to the side of the triangle, just behind the blanket stitches near the top. For the beak, sew both triangles onto the front using running stitch.

6 For the eye, sew a button onto one side of the triangle. To finish, stitch the pointed end of the fabric heart wing to the side using running stitch.

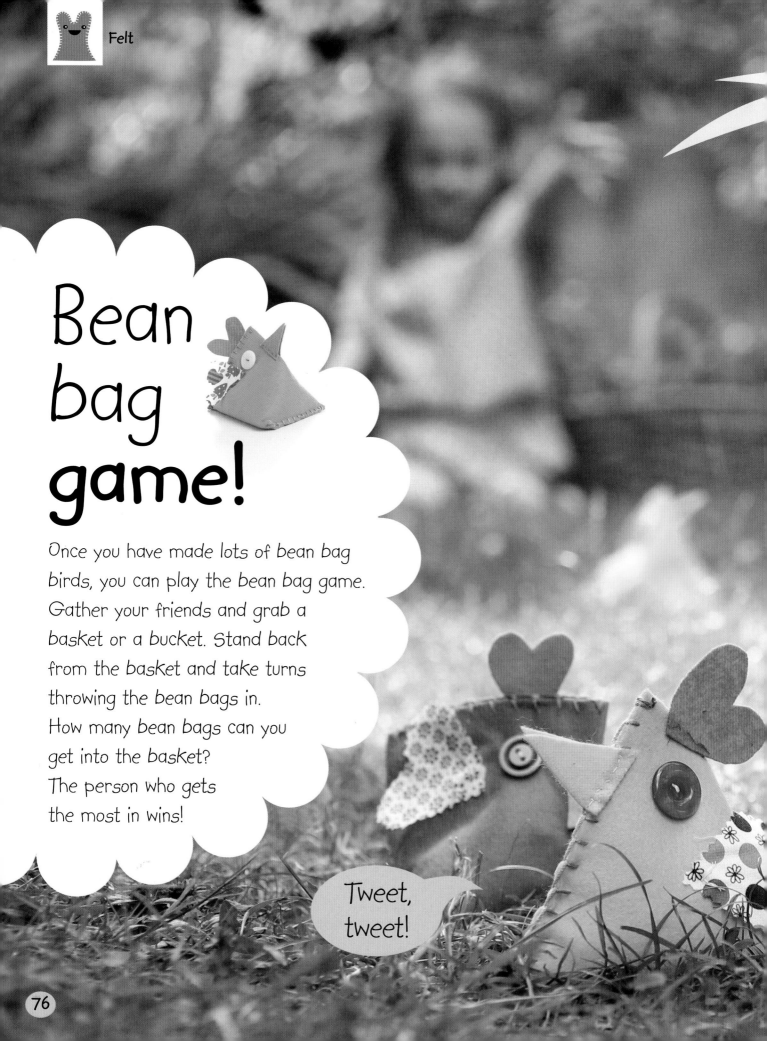

Bean bag game!

Once you have made lots of bean bag birds, you can play the bean bag game. Gather your friends and grab a basket or a bucket. Stand back from the basket and take turns throwing the bean bags in. How many bean bags can you get into the basket? The person who gets the most in wins!

Tweet, tweet!

Templates

These handy templates will help you make several of the projects.

Larry the lion mask

Trace the templates for Larry the lion mask onto tracing paper. Cut out the templates, place over construction paper, and cut out.

Find me on pages 6-7

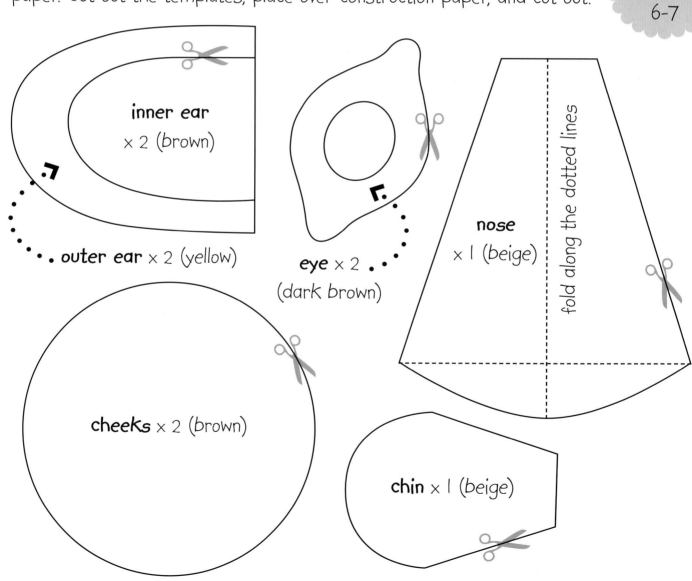

inner ear
× 2 (brown)

outer ear × 2 (yellow)

eye × 2
(dark brown)

nose
× 1 (beige)

fold along the dotted lines

cheeks × 2 (brown)

chin × 1 (beige)

Bean bag bird

Find me on pages 74-75

Trace the templates for the bean bag bird onto tracing paper. Cut out the templates; pin them to the felt and fabric before cutting out the shapes.

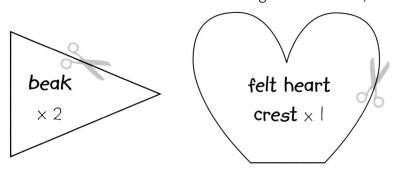

fabric heart wing x 1

beak x 2

felt heart crest x 1

Spoon dolly

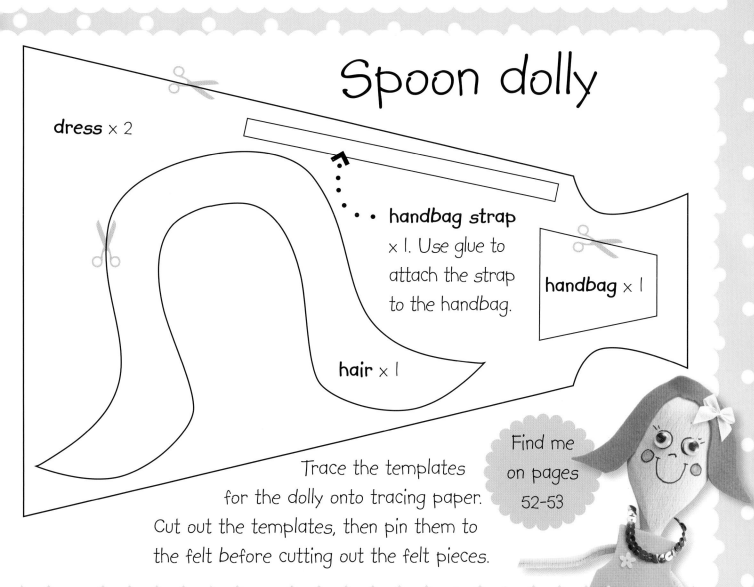

dress x 2

handbag strap x 1. Use glue to attach the strap to the handbag.

handbag x 1

hair x 1

Trace the templates for the dolly onto tracing paper. Cut out the templates, then pin them to the felt before cutting out the felt pieces.

Find me on pages 52-53

Sewing techniques

The following stitches are used in projects throughout the book.

Running stitch

This versatile stitch is used for seams, sewing fabric together, and for making gathers.

Push the needle in and out of the fabric and pull to make a stitch.

Keep the stitches and the spaces between them small and even.

Backstitch
This is a very strong stitch. It makes a continuous line of stitches so it's best for sewing two pieces of fabric securely.

Make the stitch then bring the needle back to the place where the last stitch finished.

Bring the needle out, and begin the next stitch.

Finished stitches.

Cross-stitch
This stitch is good for adding decoration to your projects.

Make a diagonal stitch. Then make another stitch on the opposite side, to make a cross shape.

Bring the needle out, ready to begin the next stitch.

Finished stitches.

Blanket stitch
This is a good stitch for making neat, decorative edges and for sewing one piece of fabric to another.

Pull the needle through the fabric. Then push the needle back through the fabric, next to the first stitch, making sure to catch the loose thread, as shown.

Push the needle up through the fabric, catching the loose thread again.

Keep the stitches neat and even.

Index

Acknowledgments

With thanks to: Jennifer Lane for additional editing, MaSovaida Morgan for assisting at a photo shoot, and Carrie Love and James Mitchem for proofreading.
With special thanks to the models: Isabella and Eleanor Moore-Smith, Cinnamon Clarke, Sol Matofska-Dyer, Miia Newman-Turner, Kaylan Patel, Isabella Thompson, Eva Menzie, Kathryn Meeker, and Jo Casey.